Unit 3

HOUGHTON MIFFLIN HARCOURT
School Publishers

ISBN-13: 978-0-547-86699-4

17 18 19 20 21   0868   21 20 19 18 17 16
4500601584   ABCDEFG

Contents

Jess Makes Gifts

by Louise Tidd
illustrated by Anne Sibley O'Brien

Jess likes to use things she has at
home to make some gifts. Jess makes
gifts for Mom, Dad, Mike, and Gram.
Jess uses different things to make those
gifts. Jess wishes that Mom, Dad, Mike,
and Gram will like the gifts she makes.

1

Jess uses paper strips and makes red roses for Mom. Jess adds stems and places bunches of roses in vases. She puts these roses on the table. Jess makes roses because Mom likes roses.

In spring, Mom will plant rose plants. Mom will make sure that the rose plants get water and sun. Mom will be glad when those roses grow. For now, Mom has these paper roses.

Jess sketches and uses brushes. She
makes a big sun, grass, a tan flag, and
golf clubs. Jess makes them because Dad
likes to play golf.

When the grass is wet, Dad cannot play golf. Dad wishes he could, but he cannot. Now Dad has these nice golf pictures that Jess made and he will smile.

Jess makes boxes of different sizes for
Mike. Jess makes five boxes red and five
boxes tan. Mike will use them as blocks.
Jess makes blocks because Mike likes to
play with them.

Jess stacks the boxes. Mike makes them crash down, and that makes him smile. Then Mike stacks the boxes and makes them fall. Another smile flashes across his face.

Jess bakes muffins for Gram because she likes muffins. Jess adds things and Mom mixes them. Jess places those muffins on dishes.

Just then, Jess heard Gram come in. Gram sat and had muffins with them. Gram thanked Jess. Jess smiled. She was thinking about what to make next.

Cooking with
Mom Fox

by Cesar Perez

illustrated by Barry Gott

Mom Fox makes good food. Mom Fox
will give classes. Mom Fox wishes little
foxes will take her classes. She hopes
those classes will be fun.

Chip, Chuck, Chet, and Chad sit in class. Mom Fox passes around boxes of mix and some cups.

"Fill a cup with mix and place the mix in those big dishes," Mom Fox tells them. "Do not spill."

Next, Mom Fox will show how to crack eggs. Chip cracks an egg, but it smashes in his hand. Chuck cracks an egg, but drops it. Chad cracks an egg, and it drips on him. Chet cracks an egg, and it splashes all over. What a mess!

Mom Fox cracks eggs for the foxes.
"What are we making?" Chip asks.
"Will it be an egg sandwich? Will it be
an egg dumpling or an egg muffin?"
Chet asks.

"You will see," Mom Fox tells them.
The foxes add milk. They whip the
milk, eggs, and mix until it fluffs up.

"Add five pinches of spice," Mom Fox
tells them. "Mix it well, too," she adds.

13

Mom Fox drops bits of the fluffed up mix on a pan. When Mom Fox finishes, she lets the foxes see.

"We made pancakes!" Chuck yells.

Mom Fox places pancakes on their plates. She dashes to get napkins. The foxes take grapes and use them to make cute fox faces on the pancakes.

"We are great at this!" Chet yells as he munches on his pancake.

"We had a great teacher," Chuck adds.

"We'll take another class," says Chet.

"Yes, we will," says Chad.

When Mom Fox heard that, she smiled.

Trains

by Prima Secunda

Would you say that playing with trains is fun? Many children think that playing with trains is fun. Children spend time making trains zip and stop on long, thin tracks.

Look at this gray train with its red, white, and blue stripes. Would you like a ride on this train?

Someone is waving. He will wait until everyone gets on. Then he will wave to say it is safe for the train to go.

People may take train rides to visit
places. This train rides on tracks that
stay close to the water.

This boy and his dad see white waves
crashing against the sand. It is fun to be
on this train as it rides on its way.

Subway trains ride on tracks under a big city. Subway trains make stops, and people get on and off. People say that subway trains are a fast way to get places in a big city.

Trains can ride on tracks that go on flat land. Trains can ride on tracks that go on high land. This train can ride on tracks along this bridge. What a nice ride people can have on this train!

Trains carry people and other things.
This train will take these logs a long way.
Trains bring us mail and food. Trains
bring many things that we use every day.

A train may pass this place. This red light flashes when a train is on its way. When this red light flashes, everyone must stop and wait as the train passes.

This train is at its last stop. Everyone must get off.

This train will wait and wait until other people can get on it. Then this train will be on its way again.

The Waiting Game

by Tyler Martin
illustrated by John Nez

Gail and Gram like playing the waiting game. Gram and Gail fix lunch and then wait for the mail. Gram and Gail say it is their best time of day!

Gram and Gail sat in a waiting spot
to play the waiting game. Gram and
Gail kept track of time with the big
clock. Gram and Gail liked to see if the
mail truck came on time. The big clock
chimed. DING!

At one o'clock, the mail truck drove
next to the mailbox. Down went the flap.
In went the mail, lots and lots of mail.
The mail truck drove away. "It's as plain
as day, you got mail today, Gram. We
win the waiting game," exclaimed Gail.

Gail ran and got the mail and gave it to Gram.

"No notes! Just junk mail and ads," said Gram.

"That is fine with me!" said Gail. Gail had such fun waiting with Gram and running to get mail in the mailbox!

Just then, Gram and Gail spotted a big
mail truck.

"Two in one day?" asked Gail.

"That is odd," said Gram.

This time the mail was a note for
them. It had lots and lots of stamps.
Gram handed Gail the note.

"What does it say?" asked Gram.

"Ray is on his way. Wait at the train at six o'clock," said Gail. Gail jumped up and gave Gram a hug and kiss. That note made Gail and Gram glad!

Gail and Gram went to wait for Ray and the train. Gail played the waiting game with Gram. Three trains passed them on the rails and didn't stop. Gram and Gail waited and waited and waited.

At last, the waiting game ended at six o'clock when a big train with red stripes stopped. Someone jumped off and ran to Gram and Gail.

Ray gave Gram, his mom, a big hug. Dad gave Gail a big hug, too!

The Shell Sheep

by Anne Miranda
illustrated by Deborah Colvin Borgo

This is a story about a sheep named
Bev. Each day Bev went to the beach and
picked up seashells. Bev collected them.

Bev liked seashells. Bev liked to
feel them. Seashells came in such neat
shapes. Bev liked to see them. Bev liked
striped shells best. Bev liked to hear the
sea when she held big shells to her ear.

Each day, when Bev got back home,
she packed seashells in boxes and stashed
them in neat lines. Bev had boxes and
boxes and boxes of seashells stacked in
her little shed.

Last week, Bev needed a rake. When
Bev reached in the shed, boxes and boxes
of shells spilled out. It seemed like a sea
of seashells! Bev had a huge problem.
Bev had way too many seashells.

Bev liked seashells, but Bev could not
keep them. The shed got full and shells
fell out. That made Bev sad.

Just then, Bev spotted a shop for sale
on the beach. That made Bev glad.

Bev had a plan. Bev named her
shop Shell World. Bev made lamps with
seashells. Bev made seashell frames. Bev
made seashell magnets and pencils.

Bev put an ad in the paper. It said:
"Sheep sells seashells at the seashore.
Sheep sells seashells cheap. This week,
free seashells with each visit!"

Lots and lots of sheep came to see Bev. Those sheep liked seashells as much as Bev did. Bev gave sheep free seashells each time one came in the shop. It made the sheep happy. That made Bev glad.

Reef Sees the Wide World

by Saturnino Romay

illustrated by Fian Arroyo

This story is about a seal named Reef. Like all seals, Reef spent his life swimming in the vast green sea. Reef could swim fast and dive deep.

41

Reef dreamed of seeing far off lands.
Reef dreamed of seeing the big wide
world, but Reef did not know which way
to go to see the wide world!

Reef just stayed close to home.

One day, Reef spotted a bird bobbing on the waves. It flapped and flapped its wings, but it could not lift off. Reef dove in and swam at top speed to it.

"May I help?" asked Reef.

Reef helped that bird get back to his stretch of beach.

"Stay with me. Take it easy. Rest until you feel well," said Reef.

"Thanks. I'm Squeak," said Squeak.

"I'm Reef," said Reef.

Squeak needed to eat and sleep. Reef fixed Squeak a big meal. Squeak ate well and then lay in a nice safe spot to sleep. Reef felt glad he had helped Squeak.

Reef spent the next day chatting with
Squeak. Squeak had seen the big wide
world. She had lots of tales to tell.

Her tales made Reef think of his
dream. He asked Squeak to help him get
to far off lands.

Reef and Squeak planned a long trip to
lands with green trees, green grass, and
beaches with white sand.

In time, Squeak felt well and her wings
felt strong. It was time for Reef to swim
away with Squeak.

Reef dove in the deep green sea. He swam as Squeak led the way. Reef and Squeak went to those far lands. At long last, Reef got his wish to see the wide world, and he saw it with his pal!

Bill E. Goat and Wise Crow

by Chenile Evans
illustrated by Lorinda Bryan Cauley

The wind felt so cold. White snow hid the green grass. Bill E. Goat did not like this cold and snow. He liked to be warm. "Hot oats will be so good," Bill E. said.

Bill E. Goat ran to the shed where he kept his oats. Bill E. could not fill his bowl with oats. He must go and get more oats at The Old Oat Shop.

He wished he did not need to go out on such a cold day.

Bill E. Goat tucked his long hair inside his yellow hat. He put on his green coat and his red mittens. He set off in snow so deep that he could not see the road. Bill E. Goat went left, but he needed to go the other way.

Bill E. Goat had made a mistake by
not going left. He went on and on in the
deep snow. He ended up in a thick grove
of trees. He did not know which way to
go. He began to get cold. Bill E. Goat
wished he had stayed home.

Just then, Bill E. Goat spotted his old
pal Wise Crow. "Can you please help me
get to The Old Oat Shop?" Bill E. asked.

"Yes, if you will bake me a big oat
cake," said Wise Crow. She winked.

Bill E. Goat smiled and nodded "Yes."

Wise Crow flapped her wings and
began to fly fast.

"I can't keep up with that speed. This
snow makes me slow," yelled Bill E. Goat.

Wise Crow came back. "We are close.
Follow me," she said.

Bill E. Goat felt so glad to be inside
The Old Oat Shop. It was nice and warm.

Nan Goat sold him three sacks of oats.
Bill E. Goat paid for them at the front of
The Old Oat Shop. Then Bill E. Goat and
Wise Crow went to bake oat cakes.

Bill E. Goat made Wise Crow a big
stack of hot oat cakes. He and Wise Crow
both ate loads of oat cakes.

Bill E. Goat told Wise Crow "Thank
you" over and over.

Mud Bugs

by Tyler Martin
illustrated by Dominic Catalano

Eb and Flo were both yellow bugs with black stripes, but you would not know it. Eb and Flo had just played in the mud. Eb and Flo had the most mud on them that two bugs could get!

Eb had clumps of mud on his feet and
hands. Eb had no yellow stripes showing.
Flo also had globs of mud on her back
and legs. Flo had one yellow stripe
showing. Both bugs needed a bath!

The bugs spotted a nice place that had a big green bathtub with no one in it. The bath seemed so warm and inviting! It had lots of foam that smelled just like roses. Will the bugs get in?

"We must test to see if bugs with mud on them will float," said Flo.

"No way! I'm going in! Bugs always float," said Eb. He dove in, but he did not float back up like he always did. Eb had to kick his feet to stay up.

Flo followed Eb in. She didn't float like she always did. She had to kick and kick to stay up as well.

"I told you so! Bugs with mud can't float. We will sink if we don't get help," said Flo.

"Hello, hello! We need help, Flo can't float!" yelled Eb.

"We both can't float!" yelled Flo.

"Hold on! Help is on its way," said a pig with long gold hair. She was holding some soap in her hand.

"I'm going to throw the soap in the
tub. It will float. Grab the soap and get
on it!" she said.

The soap splashed and landed in front
of Eb. It floated just like a boat. Eb got
on it and lifted Flo up on the soap boat.

Both bugs thanked the pig time and
time again. At last, it was time to go.
Eb and Flo went back home safe and
clean, thanks to the pig who had that
soap that floats!

What Does It Say?

by Suzanne Martinucci

That made you stop, didn't it? When you see this at street crossings, stop! Don't cross that street until you know it is safe. A grownup has that job and will tell you when it is safe.

Roz had a thought to tell Gram. Sam
and Roz wrote Gram a note. Sam helped
Roz send this note by dropping it in a
mailbox. When Gram reads it, she will
be glad that Sam and Roz care about her.
Then Gram will write back to them.

Val can send mail without a mailbox! Val sends mail on dad's laptop. Mom and Dad helped Val write to Granddad on the laptop. Then, Val pushed "Send." Her mail, with a family snapshot, was on its way in no time!

Gram and Gramps like speaking each week on the phone with their grandchild Blake. Blake began Grade 2 this week. He is telling Gram and Gramps about his classroom and his classmates.

This man speaks like you speak, but
he uses his hands, too. On this play,
someone slides into home base. This man
uses his hands to show that the man who
slid is safe.

June and her mom can not hear. Each uses her hands to speak. Mom sees what June says with her hands. Each way June holds those hands means something. Mom asks June if she had fun at camp. June tells Mom a joke.

Can you read these bumps? Maybe not, but someone who can not see can read these bumps by feeling them. These bumps are a way of writing. People who can not see can read this writing. Each set of bumps has a meaning.

Many things in this world tell us things, but do not speak. Sunrises and sunsets tell us when a day begins and ends. Rainbows do not ever speak, but rainbows tell us that the rain has stopped.

In the Grove

by Anne Miranda
illustrated by Diane Magnuson

Gramp had a nice grove of chestnut trees on his land. It was time, at last, to collect chestnuts. So, Gramp invited his grandchildren to collect and roast the ripe chestnuts on his land.

His grandsons, Edwin and James, came
to help. Edwin liked plants, but James
liked animals best. James liked hunting
insects, not picking chestnuts. Edwin
could not wait to begin! James thought
he should have stayed at home.

"When chestnuts get ripe, the pods drop. The big problem is that chestnut pods have spines. Never pick chestnuts up with your hands. Use tongs," instructed Gramp as he handed them each a big pail and tongs.

"Take care! Old Toad has his home close by," said Gramp.

"Old Toad?" asked James.

"Maybe you can spot him beneath a pod. He is this big!" said Gramp.

James began picking up pods and
placing them in his pail. He hunted for
Old Toad. When James had filled his
pail, he spotted a big black hole. He
peeked in. Old Toad peeked back.

James gave Old Toad a long look.
James was not afraid. Edwin and Gramp
ran to see Old Toad peeking at James.

"Fantastic toad!" said Edwin.

"May I hold him?" asked James.

"No, Old Toad can watch us until
we roast these chestnuts," said Gramp.
"Then he can dig back in his hole."

Gramp, James, and Edwin moved with
care around Old Toad.

Gramp opened the pods. Each pod
had chestnuts inside. He cut slits in each
nut. Then Gramp got his stove going.

Edwin and James sat and waited with
Old Toad. James felt as if they were
three pals watching Gramp.

The smell of roasting chestnuts filled
the grove. Gramp, Edwin, and James ate
hot chestnuts. Then James saw Old Toad
dig back in his toad hole. James had a
fun day after all.

Word Lists

Accompanies
Click, Clack, Moo:
Cows That Type

WEEK 1

Jess Makes Gifts

page 1

Decodable Words
Target Skill: *Base words with endings*
-s, -es
bakes, blocks, boxes, brushes, bunches,
clubs, dishes, gifts, muffins, places,
plants, roses, sizes, sketches, stacks,
strips, things, vases, wishes

Words Using Previously Taught Skills
adds, and, as, at, be, bug, but, cannot,
crash, Dad, different, face, five, flag,
flashes, get, glad, golf, Gram, grass,
had, has, he, him, his, home, in, is,
Jess, just, like, likes, made, make,
makes, Mike, mixes, Mom, next, nice,
on, paper, plant, red, rose, sat, she,
smile, smiled, spring, stems, sun, table,
tan, thanked, that, them, then, these,
thinking, those, use, uses, wet, when,
will, with

High-Frequency Words
New
another, heard, some

Previously Taught
a, about, across, because,
come, could, down, fall,
for, grow, now, of, pictures,
play, puts, sure, the, to, was,
water, what

WEEK 1

Cooking with Mom Fox
page 9

Decodable Words

Target Skill: *Base words with endings -s, -es*

boxes, chefs, classes, cups, dashes, dishes, eggs, faces, foxes, grapes, napkins, pancakes, pinches, plates, spice

Words Using Previously Taught Skills

add, adds, an, and, as, asks, at, be, big, bits, but, Chad, Chet, Chip, Chuck, class, crack, cracks, cup, cute, drips, drops, dumpling, egg, fill, finishes, five, fluffed, fluffs, Fox, fun, get, had, hand, he, him, his, hopes, in, is, it, lets, made, make, making, mess, milk, mix, Mom, muffin, munches, must, next, not, on, pan, pancake, passes, place, places, salt, sandwich, she, sit, smashes, smiled, spill, splashes, take, tells, that, them, those, toss, until, up, use, we, well, we'll, when, whip, will, wishes, with, yells, yes

High-Frequency Words

New

another, heard, some

Previously Taught

a, all, are, around, for, give, great, her, how, little, of, or, over, says, see, show, teacher, the, their, they, to, too, what, you

Trains

page 17

Decodable Words
Target Skill: *Vowel digraphs ai, ay*
day, gray, mail, may, playing, say, stay, subway, train, trains, wait, way

Words Using Previously Taught Skills
and, as, at, be, big, bridge, bring, can, child, close, crashing, dad, every, fast, flashes, flat, fun, get, gets, go, he, his, in, is, it, its, land, last, like, logs, long, make, making, must, nice, on, pass, passes, place, places, red, ride, rides, safe, sand, spend, stop, stops, stripes, take, that, then, these, thin, things, think, this, time, tracks, under, until, us, use, visit, wave, waves, waving, we, when, white, will, with, zip

High-Frequency Words
New
against, along, someone

Previously Taught
a, again, are, blue, boy, carry, children, city, everyone, food, for, go, have, high, light, look, many, off, other, people, see, the, to, water, what, would, you

WEEK 2

The Waiting Game

Decodable Words

Target Skill: *Vowel digraphs ai, ay*
day, exclaimed, Gail, mail, mailbox,
plain, play, played, playing, rails, Ray,
train, trains, wait, waited, waiting, way

Words Using Previously Taught Skills

ads, and, as, asked, at, best, big, came,
chimed, clock, Dad, didn't, ding, drove,
ended, fine, fix, flap, fun, game, gave,
get, glad, got, Gram, had, handed, his,
hug, if, in, is, it, it's, jumped, junk, just,
kept, kiss, last, like, liked, lots, lunch,
made, me, mom, next, note, notes,
o'clock, odd, off, on, passed, ran, red,
running, sat, say, six, spot, spotted,
stamps, stop, stopped, stripes, such,
that, them, then, this, three, time, track,
truck, up, we, went, when, win, with

High-Frequency Words

New
someone

Previously Taught

a, away, does, down, for,
no, of, one, said, see, the,
their, to, today, too, two,
was, what, you

The Shell Sheep
page 33

Decodable Words
Target Skill: *Vowel digraphs ee, ea*
beach, cheap, each, ear, feel, free, hear, keep, neat, needed, reached, sea, seashell, seashells, seashore, see, seemed, sheep, week

Words Using Previously Taught Skills
ad, an, and, as, at, back, best, Bev, big, boxes, but, came, day, did, fell, frames, gave, glad, got, had, held, her, home, huge, in, is, it, just, lamps, last, like, liked, lines, lots, made, magnets, much, named, not, on, packed, pencils, picked, plan, problem, rake, sad, sale, sells, shapes, she, shed, shell, shells, shop, spilled, spotted, stacked, stashed, striped, such, that, them, then, this, those, time, up, visit, way, went, when, with

High-Frequency Words
New
about, story, world

Previously Taught
a, could, for, full, happy, little, many, of, one, out, paper, put, said, the, to, too

Reef Sees the Wide World   page 41

Decodable Words
Target Skill: *Vowel digraphs ee, ea*
beach, beaches, deep, dream, dreamed,
easy, eat, feel, green, meal, needed,
Reef, sea, seal, seals, see, seeing, seen,
sleep, speed, Squeak, trees

Words Using Previously Taught Skills
and, as, asked, at, ate, back, big,
bobbing, but, chatting, close, day, did,
dive, dove, fast, felt, fixed, flapped, get,
glad, got, grass, had, has, help, helped,
him, his, home, in, is, it, its, just, lands,
last, lay, led, life, lift, like, long, lots,
made, may, named, next, nice, not,
off, on, pal, planned, rest, safe, sand,
she, spent, spot, spotted, stay, stayed,
stretch, strong, swam, swim,
swimming, take, tales, tell, thanks,
that, then, think, this, those, time, top,
trip, until, vast, waves, way, well, went,
which, white, wide, wings, wish, with

High-Frequency Words
New
about, story, world

Previously Taught
a, all, away, bird, could, far,
for, go, he, her, I, I'm, know,
me, of, one, said, saw, the,
to, was, you

Bill E. Goat and Wise Crow   page 49

Decodable Words
Target Skill: *Long o, oa, ow*
both, bowl, close, coat, cold, Crow,
follow, go, Goat, going, grove, home,
loads, oat, oats, old, over, road, slow,
snow, so, sold, told, yellow

Words Using Previously Taught Skills
and, asked, at, ate, back, bake, be,
being, big, Bill, but, cake, cakes, came,
can, can't, day, deep, did, ended, fast,
felt, fill, flapped, get, glad, grass, green,
had, hat, help, hid, him, his, hot, if, in,
inside, it, just, keep, kept, left, like, liked,
long, made, makes, mistake, mittens,
must, Nan, need, needed, nice, nodded,
not, on, paid, pal, please, ran, red, sacks,
see, set, she, shed, Shop, smiled, speed,
spotted, stack, stayed, such, thank, that,
them, then, thick, this, three, trees,
tucked, up, way, we, went, which, white,
will, wind, wings, winked, Wise, wished,
with, yelled, yes

High-Frequency Words
New
front, hair, warm

Previously Taught
a, are, began, by, could, fly,
for, good, he, her, I, know,
me, more, of, off, other,
out, put, said, the, to, was,
where, you

Mud Bugs

page 57

Decodable Words

Target Skill: *Long o, oa, ow*
boat, both, don't, dove, Flo, float,
floated, floats, foam, followed, go,
going, gold, hello, hold, holding, home,
know, most, no, roses, showing, so,
soap, throw, told, yellow

Words Using Previously Taught Skills
and, as, at, back, bath, bathtub, big,
black, bugs, but, can't, clean, clumps,
did, didn't, Eb, feet, get, globs, got,
grab, green, had, hand, hands, help,
his, I'm, if, in, inviting, is, it, its, just,
kick, landed, last, legs, lifted, like, long,
lots, mud, must, need, needed, nice,
not, on, pig, place, played, safe, see,
seemed, she, sink, smelled, splashed,
spotted, stay, stripes, test, thanked,
thanks, that, them, time, tub, up, way,
we, well, went, will, with, yelled

High-Frequency Words
New
front, hair, warm

Previously Taught
a, again, also, always,
could, he, her, I, of, one,
said, some, the, to, two,
was, were, who, would,
you

What Does It Say?

page 65

Decodable Words

Target Skill: *Compound words*

classmates, classroom, grandchild, Granddad, grownup, laptop, mailbox, rainbows, snapshot, someone, something, sunrises, sunsets, without

Words Using Previously Taught Skills

and, asks, at, back, base, Blake, bumps, but, camp, can, cross, crossings, Dad, dad's, day, didn't, don't, dropping, each, ends, feeling, fun, glad, grade, Gram, Gramps, had, hands, has, hear, helped, his, holds, home, if, in, is, it, its, job, joke, June, know, like, made, mail, man, meaning, means, mom, no, not, note, on, phone, play, pushed, rain, read, reads, Roz, safe, Sam, see, sees, send, sends, set, she, show, slid, slides, speak, speaking, speaks, stop, stopped, street, tell, telling, tells, that, them, then, these, things, this, those, time, until, us, uses, Val, way, week, when, will

High-Frequency Words

New

care, ever, thought

Previously Taught

a, about, are, be, began, begins, by, do, family, he, her, into, many, maybe, of, people, says, the, their, to, too, was, what, who

In the Grove

page 73

Decodable Words

Target Skill: *Compound words*
chestnut, chestnuts, grandchildren, grandsons

Target Skill: *Schwa vowel sound*
afraid, animals, around, collect

Words Using Previously Taught Skills
after, and, as, asked, at, ate, back, best, big, black, but, came, can, close, cut, day, dig, drop, each, Edwin, fantastic, felt, filled, fun, gave, get, going, got, Gramp, grove, had, handed, hands, has, help, him, his, hold, hole, home, hot, hunted, hunting, if, in, insects, inside, instructed, invited, is, it, James, land, last, liked, may, moved, never, nice, no, not, nut, old, on, opened, pail, pals, peeked, peeking, pick, picking, placing, plants, pod, pods, problem, ran, ripe, roast, roasting, sat, see, slits, smell, so, spines, spot, spotted, stayed, stove, take, that, them, then, these, this, three, time, toad, tongs, trees, until, up, us, use, wait, waited, watch, watching, when, with

High-Frequency Words

New
care, thought

Previously Taught
a, all, began, begin, beneath, by, could, for, have, he, I, looked, maybe, of, said, saw, should, the, they, to, was, we, were, you, your